Freshwater Aquariums

Properly Set Up Your Tank & Learn How to Make Your Fish Thrive

Anthony Daniels

Additionally, the information in the following pages is intended only for informational purposes and should thus be thought of as universal. As befitting its nature, it is presented without assurance regarding its prolonged validity or interim quality. Trademarks that are mentioned are done without written consent and can in no way be considered an endorsement from the trademark holder.

Introduction

Beautiful and fascinating are just two of the adjectives that strongly describe aquatic life. As humans, we find serenity in the calmness of the water. We find comfort in the life-giving beauty of plants. We find happiness in the marvelous lives of fishes.

These are the reasons why we are fond of keeping home aquariums. The small community inside a tank keeps our stress and anxiety away. According to psychologists, gazing at aquariums can help lessen physical and emotional pain. Aquariums positively affect human physiology such as in lowering the blood pressure. More so, they encourage creativity and boost happiness.

With all of these benefits, it is no longer surprising that fishes are the third most popular pet to keep. However, there are so much more to learn about fishes and their lives inside an aquarium.

If you want to succeed in keeping fishes as a hobby, this book is your complete map to the vast field of fishkeeping! Here, you will learn about the roots of the fishkeeping hobby.

This book is not simply about the basics. Rather, it is a complete guide in choosing a tank, types of food, equipment, decors, species, and every essential element that comprises fishkeeping as a hobby and a science.

You will also get a full view of the scientific concepts that take place beyond the human eye – such as the Nitrogen Cycle. More importantly, this book contains insightful details on how to keep an aquarium happy and healthy.

Thank you and I hope you enjoy it!

Table of Contents

Conclusion

Chapter 1: How Did Freshwater Aquariums Become Popular

History of Aquarium

Archeological evidences confirm that the Sumerians were the first aquarists in history. The Sumerians were the ancient people of Mesopotamia or the Fertile Crescent – a region between the rivers of Tigris and Euphrates.

These bodies of water provided them with vast aquatic resources. Therefore, they thought of ways to preserve the abundant supply of fishes and make it readily available for food consumption. In 2500 BC, they began maintaining artificial fish ponds to store live fishes.

Fishes were not just sources of food and livelihood during the ancient times. Rather, they were also used for their aesthetic values. Ancient Chinese are known as the first civilization to successfully breed fishes; resulting to the production of goldfish.

In the 1930s, Emperor Hongwu of the Sung Dynasty is known for harnessing the aesthetic sense of goldfish by displaying them in porcelain tubs. He started an era of using fishes as vivid and elegant ornaments reserved for the wealthy class. Later on, the Japanese copied the Chinese people's breeding methods; resulting to the creation of Carp species.

The Roman Empire is known for designing large marble tanks where they kept sea Barbels supplied by fresh seawater. They are considered as the first marine aquarists in history. These marble tanks of sea Barbels were displayed in guests' bedrooms to provide entertainment.

The Era of Naturalism

Europe was the center of ornamental fishkeeping in the 19th century due to the popularity of Naturalism. Particularly in the 1800s, naturalists and other researchers visualized and developed the concept of a balanced aquarium.

They experimented with preserving live corals, snails, fishes and other aquatic organisms inside a wooden box with a glass anterior for display and easier observation. With a good amount of sunlight, the experimental "vivatic aquariums" have successfully remained healthy due to the symbiotic relationship between the fishes and plants.

The earliest fish tank that would come close to today's modern aquariums is that of French naturalist Jeanne Power's glass aquarium. In 1832, Power used it for his experiments on aquatic organisms.

It was followed by Dr. Nathaniel Bagshaw-Ward's terrariums. In 1836, Ward began experimenting in growing live ferns and other tropical plants inside an enclosed glass; popularly known as Wardian cases.

Later on, he began adding live aquatic animals inside. It has been the first inspiration of researchers and botanists in housing plants and animals inside a tank for closer observation.

That time, the term aquarium was widely used in the field of botany which refers to a vessel used for growing aquatic plants.

In 1846, a zoologist named Anne Thynne, brought seaweed and stone corals from Torquay; and kept them in an aquarium in London. She has successfully kept the aquarium alive for three years. This made her known as the pioneer of balanced marine aquarium.

Aquariums during the Victorian Era were made of wood with a frontal glass. Later on, fish keeping has progressed as new techniques and designs were introduced.

People began constructing new aquarium models. They began exploring aquariums that are hung on a wall, fixed on a window, or merged with a birdcage.

However, the origin of the real aquarium principle, from where modern fish tanks got its inspiration, is credited to Robert Warrington. Applying the concept of plant-oxygen relationship, he theorized that fishes can live for ages inside a glass structure filled with sand, plants and snails.

He described a cycle that begins with the plants giving off oxygen to the fishes. Then, the snails would consume the decomposing plants and hatch eggs. Finally, the fishes would eat the snail eggs.

Aquariums have become more popular, especially in the United Kingdom, after they were extravagantly featured in the Great Exhibit in 1851. That year, the word "Aquarium" was first used by Philip Henry Gosse as a term referring to a container carrying aquatic animals and plants.

Two years after, the London Zoo opened its first public aquarium display due to insistent demand. It was called as the Fish House and was constructed as something similar to a greenhouse.

The British had a widespread fad about fish keeping. Soon, Paris, Naples, and Berlin adapted the London Zoo's aquarium display.

Soon enough, the Germans adapted the British hobby and even competed with them in creating more revolutionary improvements.

Later on, the United States emulated the concept of captivating fishes in an enclosed container. In 1893, aquarist societies have been founded in the United States. The United States published the world's first Aquarium Magazine in 1896 – the New York Aquarium Journal.

Through Warrington's principle, aquariums constructed by steels were successfully assembled in the 1950's. However, these aquariums didn't come with heaters and filters known today.

It was only years after when the concept of filtration became widely understood by researchers. The widespread availability of electricity after World War I has led to more revolutionary developments in aquarium.

The Emergence of Home Aquariums

In the early 1950's, fishkeeping was revolutionized by the invention of under gravel filter. It was also that time when the plastic shipping bag was developed. It allowed different varieties of fishes to be marketed and transported across the globe.

Fishes that are kept in aquariums were fed with live organisms until Dr. Baensch Atlas invented flakes in 1952. Between 1960's and 1980's, more advancement in the field of fishkeeping has been unstoppable.

The invention of more equipment – such as lights, filters, skimmers, tar, and silicone sealants – had help intricate aquatic systems thrive under different circumstances.

At the latter part of the twentieth century, a Japanese designer and aquarist named Takashi Amano had a big contribution in the area of aquatic design. He has established a unique style for an aquascape layout which imitates nature's appearance.

He incorporated Japanese gardening concepts like Zen and Wabi-Sabi in his aquarium. He used floating and flowering plants as decors inside his tanks.

He also thought of controlling algae growth by using shrimps. Hobbyists and fish keepers were inspired by this layout. Soon, home aquariums became aesthetically pleasing aquatic compositions.

Since then, the hobby of fishkeeping has flourished. In 1996, fishkeeping has become the second most popular hobby in the United States; next to stamp collecting.

The fishes that once were just reserved for the wealthy and privileged have become very common to more households. The delighting beauty of keeping a home aquarium has finally been discovered by more people.

Chapter 2: How to Properly Set Up Your Aquarium

Tank Size Does Matter

Before setting up your own Freshwater Aquarium, keep in mind that tank size does matter and it is crucial. It is the basic element that will affect your time, effort, materials, and budget. Tank size and shape will vary depending on your personal taste and choice.

However, you may want consider the following factors to help you organize your thoughts.

Determine the area or space in your home where you would like to place the aquarium. Think of a size that would complement the aesthetic design of that space.

When carefully planned, an aquarium can add a magical transformation to your home's aesthetic values. Be sure to pick a spot that is out of the direct sunlight; since sunlight can affect the water temperature and increase the growth of algae.

Think of the number of fishes and kind of species that you want to keep. Obviously, the more or larger the species are, the wider the tank should also be.

Typically, you may follow the ratio of 1 inch of fish is to 1 gallon of water. There are fishes that grow in only an inch or two.

If you choose that kind of species and decide to keep just a few inhabitants, a standard size (20-40 gallon fish tank) will be enough.

It is important to know that smaller tanks are not recommended for novice hobbyists. Changes in water chemistry can bring harmful effects that are difficult to minimize in smaller tanks.

If you want to house more fishes and choose tropical species that grow more in length, you may opt for a larger tank. There is no limit in choosing a tank size.

There are even aquariums that measure as large as 180-gallon (72" x 24" x 25"). However, keep in mind that the maintenance of larger tanks may also become overwhelming in the long run.

Choosing a Substrate

Consider the kind of substrate that you want to use. Substrate refers to the material mantled at the bottom of the tank.

The substrate can have an impact on filtration, water chemistry, and the inhabitants' health. More so, it can extensively affect the tank's aesthetics.

There are several choices of substrates such as sand, pebbles, neon-colored gravel, marbles, and corals. Among these, gravel is the most common.

It comes in different sizes and colors which are mostly vivid; adding more life to the aquarium. Gravel also contains a nutrient called laterite which may be beneficial to the plant's growth.

However, there are species that do not suit a gravel bottom. If you want to keep a Corydoras catfish, for example, a gravel bottom must be crossed out of your options.

This species tend to hunt underneath in search of food; something that would be difficult to do in a sea of gravel. More so, sharp gravel may damage their barbels.

Even the popular home aquarium star, gold fish, may be put in danger as it can swallow pieces of gravel. Although the gravel can still be removed from the throat, doing so might still put the gold fish in a lot stress.

Sand may not be as popular as gravel but it provides easy maintenance when used correctly. Dirt particles would not sift through underneath but would just rather stay on top.

Just like gravel, sand also contains laterite that provides benefits for live plants. When using sand, opt for the coarser and medium grains.

Fine grains of sand hinder root development of live plants and have higher chances of becoming anaerobic. Also, be careful in planting live plants through the sand as the laterite may blur the water.

Big rocks and marbles can also be used as substrates as they have good decorative effects. However, it would be better if rocks remain as embellishments instead.

Bacteria can easily grow on them and there are times when fishes get stuck between these rocks.

Aragonite and corals may look attractive when used as substrates. However, these materials are not recommended as they lower the water's pH level.

Unless you are thinking of maintaining a brackish aquarium, a low pH level is something to avoid. Corals can easily attract dirt; affecting the water quality.

Between corals and aragonite, the latter is much recommended by aquarists but its downside would be its very expensive price.

Going for a bare bottom, on the other hand, requires more analysis as it is not suitable to every kind of inhabitants.

Freshwater tanks are good enough for bare bottoms but saltwater tanks are not.

In terms of plant decors, tanks that contain corals can survive in naked bottoms but real plants obviously can't. However, if you only want to keep the famous gold fish, going bare-bottom may be suitable for easier cleaning.

Since gold fish is one untidy species, it requires constant cleaning. Therefore, a bare bottom may become an advantage.

Live Plants Vs Fake Plants

We rarely see a freshwater aquarium that does not come with a plant decor. Due to the fresh look it provides, plant is the top choice for fish tank embellishments.

It makes an aquarium more alive as it mimics the genuine feel of nature. It also provides hiding spots for the fishes; making them feel secure.

Most fish owners prefer plastic plants for their aquariums. First of all, artificial plants provide easy maintenance as their leaves do not fall and wither.

Just like live plants, they also give the inhabitants a space for hiding. Artificial plants are made to appear more vivid than live ones.

However, the most common artificial plants are made of a lightweight bottom. As time goes by, it becomes a pain in the eye as it would usually float in the water.

There are some fake plants, though, that are made of heavy bottoms. However, they would cost much than the lightweight ones. Since artificially colored plants are designed to look more vibrant, the cheaper varieties can look unnatural.

Live plants may not be as vibrant as the fake ones. However, they provide benefits that artificial plants cannot duplicate.

Live plants improve the quality of water and provide a balanced ecosystem for the inhabitants. Obviously, they can provide a natural habitat for the fishes. They provide substantial levels of oxygen that help the fishes breathe.

They help the pH level rest on its normal range. However, when real plants die, they cause a spike in the tank's nitrogen level.

This eventually stresses the fishes. Uncontrolled and high levels of nitrogen will become lethal. Therefore, live plants require more maintenance and constant observation than fake ones.

In terms of cost, real plants are more expensive than artificial plants.

Fishes would not really care if the plants around them are live or fake. They would not even be able to tell the difference.

Plants, whether real or artificial, provide the same function to the inhabitants –realistic environment and shelter.

Choosing the Decors

Fish tank adornments can make your aquarium stand-out. They are like accessories to a boring outfit; they can add instant magic to the tank's over-all aesthetic.

They can set the mood and theme. More so, they also provide safety and comfort to the inhabitants.

In choosing your decors, keep a theme that you want to carry out and stick with it. Example, if you want a nature-themed aquarium that resembles real aquatic habitat, adorn the tank with decors akin to what can be seen in nature.

These may include live plants to provide greenery and rock formations to mimic the ocean.

You may also adorn the tank based on your personality. Example, if you have a fun personality, you may add blasts of colors in the aquarium; such as colored plants or multi-colored rocks.

Complement them with the inhabitants by choosing rainbowfish or clown fish. You may also decorate the tank based on its constant viewers.

Example, if you have a little girl in the house who serves as the fishes' constant audience, entertain her by creating a fairytale-themed aquarium. Put a castle with holes where fishes can swim through.

If you do not want to put a castle, you may simply put a castle background. Add fairy objects or mermaid accessories.

While it may be tempting to gather possible decors and accessories in and out of the house (the beach, for example), be careful in doing so; as these accessories may contain parasites that can harm the inhabitants.

More so, avoid decorating the tank with copper and painted objects. These contain poisonous chemicals. Avoid objects with sharp edges as well.

Lighting the Tank

Just like any other community, lighting is also essential in an aquatic habitat. Aside from good quality water, good lighting boosts the plants' natural growth.

Scientifically, light is crucial as plants undergo photosynthesis to live and remain healthy. Generally, plants will do fine in a moderate light.

However, there are plants that require more intense lighting than other species; such as plants with a touch of red in the stem or leaves.

Light also affects the fishes' health and enrich their colors. More so, good lighting allows you to closely observe the activities in the tank; making it easier to prevent if there are any arising problems.

Now that you have probably thought on the kind of fishes and plants that you want, choosing the type of light to be used will be based on these factors.

The most traditional lighting used by aquarists is the tubular Standard Fluorescent Light. First off, this type is a lot cheaper and easily available.

Despite the cheap price, it can provide good lighting to support plant growth. There are also several choices of a fluorescent light.

There are types that are warmer, types that give off white and blue light mimicking marine habitat, types that give deep blue shade mimicking deep underwater, and types that are called plant bulbs which is beneficial for photosynthesis.

You may easily purchase one that complements the theme you have chosen. However, this type of light does not lasts long compared to others; so you may need to replace it often. Also, it emits more heat and does not provide a gleam similar to that of the ocean water.

Another type of lighting is the Compact Florescent Light. Unlike the standard one that comes in a single tube, the compact type combines two or more tube bulbs for better lighting. It has the same advantages that come in a standard fluorescent – cheaper, easily available, easy to operate, and has a wide selection of colors.

However, a single compact lighting fixture can do the job of a two individual tube fluorescent. Therefore, a compact type is more space-saving. Metal Halide is also an option for freshwater aquariums because it mimics natural sunlight.

It is especially recommended for very large tanks; something deeper than 24 inches. It consists of halide salt and mercury vapor.

Physically, it has a main bulb that is connected to another arc bulb through wires. The vapor and salt produces light as electricity passes through the arc bulb.

It gives a shimmering effect to the water as the light deeply passes through the tank. It does not require constant replacement because it is long-lasting. However, this type may be quite expensive.

In this modern era of fishkeeping, an innovative type of lighting has been recently introduced. Most modern tanks already use a LED (Light Emitting Diode).

This newcomer can benefit both real and artificial plants as it provides a pure and deeply penetrating light. It comes in varying colors that mimic a natural freshwater hue or complement the fishes and plants' natural glow.

It is also more energy-saving and does not give off too much heat. Just like a metal halide, it provides shimmer on the water similar to an ocean's shiny glow. However, an LED is also expensive.

Other Aquarium Products and Accessories

Aside from the aesthetics, keeping an aquarium must also involve mechanical and scientific equipment to ensure that everything is working properly.

A heater ensures that the tank's temperature remains stable. Fish do not produce their own body heat unlike human and other mammals.

Therefore, it is important to maintain a stable tank temperature because the fishes rely on it to maintain their own body heat. There are two types of heater, the submersible and external.

Do not use a heater that is too large for your tank as it may cause heating problems.

A thermometer works hand in hand with the heater. Changes in the water temperature may cause possible problems to the tank.

Unfortunately, these changes cannot be observed just by watching over the tank. You need a thermometer to track the temperature.

There are different types of thermometer. Standing or floating thermometers allow you to directly measure the water temperature by placing it inside the aquarium.

There are thermometer types that simply float in the water, weighted types that sink at the bottom of the water, one that uses a suction cup, and a hanging type.

These are inexpensive types and not affected by room temperature. However, these types may be difficult to read as the scale is much smaller than the others.

Also, these are made of glass so they can possibly be broken especially if you have larger fishes. Another type of thermometer is the digital thermometer.

It comes with a reader that is placed inside the tank. The temperature it reads will be reflected on the small screen device that is placed outside.

There are very modern models that come with an alert tone that alarms when the temperature goes above or below the expected level. This type can be very efficient as it can provide the most accurate reading.

However, it is the most expensive type. A LCD or Stick-on Thermometer is also available.

This type is the most commonly used as it is inexpensive, versatile, easy to use and can be easily placed in any location. However, it can be less accurate than the digital type and can be hard to read in low-light.

A filtration system or simply filter is another important accessory in setting up a freshwater aquarium. It removes harmful chemicals, fish manure, floating particles, left over feeds, decaying organic materials and other toxins from the water.

When left unremoved, these toxins can cause ammonia spike which can cause death to the fishes. You might say that you can always conduct a cleaning routine every day.

However, deep-cleaning can actually cause shock and stress to the fishes. A filter helps in cleaning the tank without the stressful process.

There are basically three types of filtration: Chemical, Mechanical, and Biological. Through a mechanical filtration, the water is pushed to a medium that acts as a strainer.

The strainer can come in a form of pads, filter floss, or a sponge. It sips the free-floating particles present in the water without interrupting the water chemistry.

It comes in different types and sizes. Extra fine mechanical medium can remove extra small particles including bacteria and parasites. A coarse to medium grade type can remove the most visible debris.

A very coarse medium grade type absorbs extra-large debris. The larger the medium is, the larger the particles that it can extract. The larger medium can also be easier to clean than a fine one.

A biological filter helps in breaking down bacteria and other microorganisms. In turn, these bacteria and microorganisms will be converted into less harmful by-products.

A biological filter also comes in different types. A smaller one can last for 2-4 years and is the best option if you have a smaller tank.

It may be small in size but it is reliable enough in absorbing a lot of bacteria. A plastic biological filter, on the other hand, may not have a wide surface area. However, it does not clog easily and can even survive longer than the other types.

A chemical filter removes toxins from the water through chemical resins and activated carbons. This type of filter is not commonly used compared to a mechanical and biological one.

However, it can also be a good accessory in maintaining good water quality as it removes unwanted particles and matter that adheres to it.

Types of Water

In setting up a freshwater aquarium, it is common for hobbyists to use tap water because of its easier availability. Tap water is cleansed using several chemicals to kill the bacteria and make it safe for human consumption.

However, these chemicals, such as chlorine and chloramine, can harm the fishes. If using tap water, you must check first its nitrate level, gH, kH and pH level.

You must also clean the water using a chloramine remover or dechlorinator.

Tap water may work fine but it can still be disadvantageous to the fishes. The best option you have in lieu of the tap water is spring water.

When choosing a brand of spring water, make sure that it is not distilled as it means that the water has already been stripped off of minerals.

To ensure that the water is free from harmful substances, such as mercury, copper or zinc, and that it is detoxified, you may use a water conditioner. It neutralizes chlorine and other unwanted materials in the water.

It is a bottled solution that is added in the water, especially if you really have no choice but to use tap water. A typical water conditioner is recommended to be used in a ratio of 2 teaspoons per 10 gallons of water

Setting up the tank

After a thorough planning on the materials, theme, size, and accessories that you want for your freshwater aquarium, it is now time to set it up.

Clean the tank first using a clean soft sponge and warm water to erase extra residue and get rid of harmful chemicals in the tank, if there are any. Do not use any kind of soap in cleaning the tank as it may leave residues that may harm the fishes.

Next, set up the tank in a steady base. The tank itself may be carried easily but once it is filled with water, it becomes heavy. So, be sure to place it in a stable base that is strong enough to hold the aquarium's weight.

If you are placing the aquarium beside the wall, make a 5' allowance to make enough room for the filter.

Fill in the tank with the gravel or your chosen substrate; then, add the other decorations. Ensure of the cleanliness of the materials that must be submerged inside the aquarium.

In cleaning the decors, you may simply wash them off over running water. Other embellishments like driftwood, rocks, or shells may need extra scrubbing to get rid of parasites and dirt.

In cleaning the substrate like gravel, simply submerge it in a bucket of water to remove dirt; then, strain to remove other unwanted particles.

By this time, the live plants may be added in the aquarium. Be sure to wash them first under running water to get rid of unwanted parasites and deposits.

Check if there are decaying roots and leaves on the plants. Begin placing the taller plants at the back area followed by the smaller ones at the front. Ideally, these plants will hide the other equipment.

Arrange the wood or rock decorations as desired. Then, put a base fertilizer if you are using live plants. Add in the substrate; make a sloping direction towards the back of the tank.

Set up the other equipment. Assemble and install the filter behind the tank.

Install the thermometer in your desired position or in a spot that would allow easier monitoring. Set up the heater and wait for about 15 minutes or until its thermostat has adapted to the water temperature.

Install the light and hood in the aquarium. Be sure that the power cords will not get wet. After that, turn the equipment on to see if everything is working properly.

Next, add in the spring water. To avoid disarranging the substrate and other decors, place a saucer or plate on top of the gravel.

Then, pour the water directly onto the plate. If you have no choice but to add tap water, make sure to use a water conditioner.

Leave the set-up for a day or so until the nitrogen cycle has completed before adding the fish. Once the temperature has stabilized, turn off the electric equipment.

Then, add the first fish (or two). Wait for another six weeks or until the nitrite and ammonia levels have dropped to zero before adding all the other additional fishes.

Chapter 3: What Kind of Fish Should You Get

Buying a healthy fish

Searching for the perfect pet to occupy your tank must be done in a thorough planning. Of course you want something that is worth your money, time and effort.

The first step into buying a healthy fish is making sure that you are transacting in a reputable pet shop. First of all, do a research about fish tanks and ask the staff some questions related to what you have learned.

If they know what they are talking about, then, you are dealing with credible people. Observe around the store.

Look closely into the displayed tanks to see if there are dead fishes floating in there. A good store would not allow dead fishes into the displays, especially if it is co-inhabiting with live ones.

Observe if there are fishes that have small white spots or other symptoms of sickness. Do not buy a fish that comes from a tank with sick inhabitants.

Tinted water may also be a sign that the tank houses a sick fish. To ensure that the fish is healthy, it must have the following characteristics: clear eyes, active and alert movement but not too hyperactive, steady breathing, fins must be in good shape and condition, must not be bloated, must not be slimy and must have a healthy color.

More importantly, it must look clean and not have any blemishes in the body as these can be signs of stress or bacterial infection.

Once you have decided and picked a healthy fish to buy, ask the staff to add more water in the fish bag if you are going to drive for 15 minutes or more.

Fish Quantity

It is safe to say that more fishes in the tank provide more entertainment. However, you should always remember that overpopulation would possibly result to a disaster.

In determining the number of fishes to house in your aquarium, the basic ratio to follow is an inch of fish is to one gallon of water. While this rule might give a rough estimate for a good start, it must also be considered that fishes would grow as time goes by.

Therefore, in using this rule, calculate using the typical adult size of a fish. Consider the shape of the fish as well.

It is wrong to assume that the tank's size is equivalent to the volume of water it can hold. Example, a five-gallon tank filled with plants, gravel and other decors does not really hold 5 gallons of water.

Actually, there must be a 10-15 percent difference between the tank size and water volume.

Another way to determine the number of fishes that a tank can hold is by calculating the tank's surface area. To calculate the surface area of a tank, multiply its length by its width.

This method uses a ratio of 1 inch of fish is to 12 square inches of the tank. This ratio applies only to slimmer fishes.

For wide-bodied fishes, the ratio must be an inch of fish per 20 square inches. This rule would work better than the one-inch rule if the aquarium is a non-standard size.

Another method to determine an aquarium's substantial population is by calculating the ratio of fish weight by the water volume. Typically, the ratio must be one gram of fish is to 4 liters of water.

Community fish and aggressive fish

One of the most exciting parts of setting up an aquarium is choosing the fishes to keep. There are wide choices as there are literally a thousand species of fishes.

However, choosing the inhabitants to shelter in your aquarium is not as easy as picking up whatever you fancy. There are fishes that go peacefully with everyone else while there are also some that come as a threat to others. Freshwater species are categorized based on these temperaments.

Community fishes are those that are considered peaceful. They are harmonious in nature and can be mixed well with almost every species.

They behave well when grouped with other fishes belonging to the same species. However, there are some community fishes that can become aggressive when kept alone; such as tiger barbs and serape tetras.

Although they may be aggressive when alone or kept in pairs, they can still be peaceful when kept in large groups. It is recommended to shelter them in groups of 4-6 with their other co-species.

Examples of community fishes are danios, guppies, platies, swordtails, mollies and majority of tetras.

The next category is the semi-aggressive type. These are peaceful fishes that can still display aggressiveness under some circumstances.

If you want to keep this type of fish, make sure that there is only one semi-aggressive male in the community. Also, be sure to provide more hiding places inside the aquarium. This way the smaller fishes can protect themselves in case the semi-aggressive displays threat and aggression.

If you want more than one semi-aggressive fishes, make sure that your tank is large enough because they can be territorial. They will get along fine as long as there is a spot that they can consider as their territory.

Examples of semi-aggressive fishes are eels, loaches, barbs and gouramis.

Aggressive fishes, on the other hand, have wild temperaments. They are hardly compatible with other species.

They exude a strong territorial aggressiveness especially if a male fish is mixed with another male fish. Fishes belonging in this category may be mixed with other co-species but are still better kept alone.

They also tend to be aggressive on fishes that look similar to them.

Housing aggressive fishes may require more expertise that is why they are not recommended for newbie aquarists. Examples of aggressive fishes are Plecostomus, large catfish, and most cichlids like African and Oscar.

Fish Compatibility

In order for your little freshwater community to stay serene, the inhabitants must be compatible with each other; they must co-exist peacefully. As previously mentioned, there are species that can go along well with any other species while there are some that cannot.

Here are some specific examples of popular tropical fishes that are and are not compatible with each other.

Guppies can be grouped with other small fishes like Platties and Mollies. They prefer alkaline water.

Therefore, these peaceful fishes are not advisable to be mixed with others that prefer acidic and soft water.

Barbs and Cichlids should not be mixed together. The latter have long fins and the former is a known fin nipper.

Guppies should also not be mixed with fin nippers such as gouramis. If keeping guppies, follow the ratio of two females per one male to help maintain peace in the community.

An angelfish may also be meant for schooling but with some exceptions. It cannot be mixed with neon tetras and guppies as it may show aggression around these species.

Female bettas are good for schooling but take caution among other species that may nip at their fins. Male bettas, on the other hand, must be the only betta in the aquarium. Better yet, it must be sheltered in a separate tank.

Chapter 4: How to Properly Feed Your Fish

Different types of feed

Feeding your aquarium inhabitants is a way of interacting with them. It strengthens the bond between the fishes and the owner.

However, feeding is not as simple as letting them eat what is available inside the house. They, too, have specific nutritional needs.

The most common type of feed available in the market is dry food like the popular pellet and flakes. Pellets take longer time to dissolve in the water; thus, its vitamin content can also be retained for a longer period of time.

Pellets do not usually mess the water; giving the owner an easier maintenance. Pellets are easier to swallow.

However, it can expand in size when soaked in the water for a long time. When the fishes eat too much expanded pellets, their digestive system can become stressed.

There are also worse cases where overfeeding of pellets resulted to death.

Flakes, on the other hand, do not expand in size even after being soaked in the water. It is a digestion-friendly food.

However, unlike pellets, flakes are thinner and softer. It may not expand in size but it is still easily dissolves in water. Therefore, the nutrient value can be easily washed.

It can also transform into powdered or smaller pieces which makes the water blurry.

Other examples of dried fish food are granules, crisps and discs. Granules are similar to pellets but just come in smaller sizes.

Crisps are the identical version of flakes. It also holds the same nutrients as flakes but just comes in a different shape.

Crisps come as thin tablet-like form; which makes it less messy than flakes. Discs are plant-based food that also come in thin-sized tablets and sinks at the bottom of the water.

In choosing feed for the aquatic pets, be sure to check the ingredients first. As a rule, avoid any feed that contain tons of carbohydrates.

Carbohydrates may come in the form of potato protein, wheat flour, inositol and feeding oatmeal. Instead, choose feeds that contain spirulina (nutritious algae), shrimp meal, fish meal, and earthworms which is high in Vitamin D and protein.

Aside from the dried food, there are still other varieties of feed. Example of these is gel food.

It is similar to dried food in terms of ingredients but has less preservative. Compared to flakes, gel food expires longer.

Frozen dry foods are also available in the market. These are the kinds of food that went through a sublimation process.

Freezing is a good preservation. However, the vitamins and nutritional contents are dissolved as the food undergoes the process.

If you would like to use this type of feed, be sure to drench it first in water. Doing so will prevent bladder sickness and help the fishes digest the feed smoothly.

Vacation blocks, or vacation food are also available. As the name suggests, this type of food is supposed to feed the fishes for a week's time.

It can be left in the aquarium for five days to one week; especially if you are out on a vacation.

This type of feed is made with little amount of real food that is why it also has little or almost no nutritional value. More often than not, the fishes won't even be able to recognize it as food.

So, they end up just ignoring the feed. As a result, the feed dissolves in the water causing a foul odor.

Live food is also an option for feeding the inhabitants. However, due to the introduction of modern feeds, live food is just mostly considered as treats nowadays.

Examples of these are cyclops, blood worms, black worms, ghost shrimp, brine shrimps, and copepods.

Actual or live food may sound perfect as its nutritional value does not undergo any process. It is still there, intact and not lost in the actual food.

It also stimulates the fishes' hunting instincts and appetite. However, it also has its own share of downsides including its minimal availability.

It is quite difficult to look for pet shops or stores that carry such feeds. Hunting on your own is a bad idea either as you may pick ones that contain pathogens; especially black worms that are often caught in dirty water and sewage.

Quantity and Schedule of Feeding

Fishes always take advantage in terms of eating. They eat whenever food is available – hungry or not.

Observe that when the fishes get used to seeing you feed them, they would always get your attention whenever you are around. They would show off their jumping moves in the water, for example.

While it is tempting to let them gobble their food up any time of the day, doing so may cause overfeeding. Contrary to some popular myths, fishes won't explode once over fed.

However, overfeeding may still cause health problems including the risk of developing hepatic lipidosis or a fatty liver disease.

It can also cause rotting of their fins and may bring them stress. More so, feeds that are left unconsumed in the water can affect the fishes' health.

Unconsumed feed in the water will turn into harmful by-products that lead to uncontrolled growth of mold, blurry water and growth of algae.

In terms of frequency, fishes will generally do fine with a single feeding per day. Nevertheless, there is nothing wrong if you want to feed them more than once a day.

Just make sure to feed them in small amounts regardless of the feeding frequency. Juvenile fishes need more frequent small feedings, though. Feed them six times a day.

In terms of schedule, there are really no rules to follow. However, if you are keeping nocturnal feeders, it is obviously necessary to give them special treatment in terms of feeding schedule.

Give them food as late as possible in the night or just before turning off all the lights.

In terms of the amount of feed, it is recommended to give them smaller amounts. To make it accurate, there are several factors and rules to follow.

If you only have a single fish in the tank, it is recommended to feed it with small pieces of flakes or 3-5 big pieces of pellets. Usually, a single fish can consume this amount within 10 to 30 seconds.

If your tank is full of fishes, feed them the amount that they can consume within a minute. Even 1 or 2 pinches can already be enough for several fishes.

There is no need to re-feed them as long as everyone gets their share; 1 or 2 pieces of pellets per fish can already be enough.

For the first few weeks, follow these rules and observe the fishes' eating habit. Ideally, unconsumed or leftover feed should not be present in the water. If you observe that the fishes are already ignoring the leftover feed, then, it is a sign that you are giving too much.

Use your fingers in feeding akin to sprinkling. Do not pour the feed directly from the bottle or bag into the tank. This often leads to overfeeding.

Giving Treats

No matter how fishes seem to find happiness and contentment with dry feed, they still jump in excitement every time they are given live food as treats. Commercial feed may be designed to provide adequate nutrients for the fishes.

However, live food also has large amount of nutrients and unlike commercial food, these nutrients have not been processed or altered. When in the wild, freshwater fishes have a wide variety of diet.

Therefore, you also have several kinds of live food to choose from.

One of their most favorite live foods is the black worm. However, you should be very careful on getting black worms for feeding.

If not properly cleaned, they can be carriers of parasitic and bacterial infection as they mostly live in filthy places and thrive in animal manure. To ensure the cleanliness of black worms, make sure to buy from a trusted pet shop.

Just like in purchasing live fishes, observe the quality of water where that black worms are kept. The water should be nothing but clear.

If it is not, do not buy from that store; or do not purchase a black worm taken from that water.

Once purchased, you still have to clean the black worm by rinsing it 3-4 times a day. Then, put them in a large water container.

Then, let the container rest in the refrigerator overnight. Check the container the next morning.

Observe the water quality. If it is clear, then, it means that the worms have already been thoroughly cleaned. If not, continue the rinsing process.

Another favorite live food of fishes is Brine Shrimps or Artemia. Brine shrimps can be consumed live or frozen.

The taste of a frozen one varies depending on the diet that the shrimp had. But no matter what flavor or brand it is, even small inhabitants would like nibbling these.

There are several pet shops that sell brine shrimps. However, these can be quite expensive.

Water flea or Daphnia is also an option. It is a good choice in terms of nutrients and it is safer than black worms because they are known as non-carriers of diseases. Daphnia can also be a part of the fish tank. It can live with the other inhabitants until eaten.

Other good choices for treats are white worms, micro-worms, earth worms, mosquito larvae, maggots, flies and vinegar eels. Being their only chef, your fish tank inhabitants will thank you for giving them different tastes and flavors once in a while.

You may feed them small amounts of live food at a time; once to thrice a week is fine.

Over feeding the fishes with live food can result to intestinal problems due to its rich properties. Also, you may want to crush them in smaller pieces. Just like in dry flakes or pellets, feed them in only what they can finish in a minute.

Feeding and Eating Habit of Fishes

The eating habit of fishes is one factor that determines the kind of food they need. In terms of eating, fishes can be divided into three categories; namely the top feeders, middle feeders and bottom feeders.

The top feeders are recommended to be fed with floating pellets or flakes because they turn their mouths up and move up to the surface of the water when trying to eat. The most popular examples of top-feeders are gouramies and hatchetfish.

Bottom feeders have down-turned mouths and moves down to the bottom of the water when trying to feed. It is best to give them discs or tablets or other heavier food that will sink under the tank. Popular examples of bottom feeders are loaches.

Meanwhile, fishes that are somewhere in the middle or basically have mouths turned forward are called middle feeders. They are best fed with granules or essentially smaller pellets that either float or sink. Examples of these are Cory Catfish and Plecos.

To know the proper type of food preferred by your fishes, observe the area where they like to eat. Basically, the rule is to give floating food for top-feeders, sinking food for bottom feeders; and food that are either sinking or floating for middle feeders.

Nevertheless, bottom feeders can also cope with sinking food; but not with floating ones.

Chapter 5: Common Fish Illnesses and How to Treat Them

It is always quite alarming when you notice one of your fishes get ill or sick; especially if you are a novice hobbyist.

The most worrisome thing is perhaps the fact that fishes are delicate in nature.

Therefore, a prolonged illness may not only cost the fish's life but affect the entire aquarium community as well.

Ichthyophtirius

One of the most common illnesses that a freshwater fish may attract is Ichthyophtirius or simply ich. It is also known as white spots due to the small white dots on the skin.

These slightly raised white spots akin to salt grains are actually parasites.

Fishes affected by this bacterial infection are observed to be scratching their bodies on objects due to skin itching.

They are always out of breath. The white spots are visible in the entire body but shows greater focus on the fins and gills.

It is commonly caused by poor water quality and raised pH levels. More so, it commonly happens upon introducing new fishes in the tank.

The first step in treating this disease is cleaning the tank's water. After that, you may purchase medications available in the pet stores.

The medication usually comes in tablet forms that are dropped in the water; or it might be an aquarium salt.

Remove the carbon filter when giving medications as it may just absorb the medicine.

This disease usually takes 5 days before completely treated. However, it is better to treat it as soon as possible because it can be contagious.

To avoid such illness, maintain clean water and put new fishes in a solo tank first before introducing them in the main aquarium.

Fishes that are stressed are also prone to being infected with this disease.

Fin Rot

As the name suggests, it is a bacterial infection that eats up or rots the fins of a fish.

Other physical symptoms may include less movement and just lying at the bottom of the tank.

It commonly occurs alongside an Ich. This disease is a result of unsanitary conditions including poor water quality.

It may also be caused by poor nutrition and vitamin deficiency. Other cases may be caused by bullying especially if there are fin-nipping fishes in the tank.

Cleaning the water is a necessary step in treating this disease.

There are also appropriate medicines such as Tetracycline and other antibiotics available in the local pet stores.

Also, give the fish a more nutritious diet but do not overfeed.

Fish Fungus

Fish Fungus is also known as Cotton Wool; taken from the white or grayish cotton-like patches that appear on the body of an infected fish. It starts out as small patches of infection on certain areas especially the mouth or fins and spreads all over the body.

It is a parasitic infection that is commonly caused by Saprotrophs or water molds. Saprotrophs are supposedly unthreatening; in fact they even help the habitat by eating on wastes.

However, under undesirable circumstances such as when the fish is weak and stressed, it takes advantage and grabs this opportunity to absorb the nutrients and proteins in a fish's body.

Once diagnosed with Fish Fungus disease, the fish must be transferred immediately into a quarantine tank.

Immediate action is necessary as the disease is not only contagious but can also become fatal once the infection spreads all throughout the body.

For the treatment, ask your local pet store to give you antibiotic or fungicidal; preferably something that contains formalin and malachite green. These come in tablet forms.

Add one tablet for every 10 gallons of water. Since the parasites are caused by unclean water, it is necessary to include water changing as part of the treatment.

Anchor Worm

Anchor worm is a parasitic disease that is caused by crustacean worms by burrowing into the skin and staying in the muscles until they lay eggs. It is characterized by white-green worms that protrude from the skin.

The spot where the worm attaches to the skin will also become red and inflamed.

Other symptoms are grasping for breath and skin discomfort. To kill the parasites, dip the fish in a saltwater bath for five minutes; and thrice a day.

Anti-parasitic medicines such as potassium permanganate, clout and formalin are also available in the local pet stores. You may also want to remove the worms by using a tweezer. Gently pull the worms out by gripping it as close to the skin as possible.

Body Flukes

Flukes are flatworms that are approximately 1 mm long. These flatworms are commonly present in aquariums and are supposedly harmless.

However, when undesirable sanitary conditions happen, the fishes become stressed. The flatworms take advantage of this stress to transmit bacterial infections.

Unnecessary habitat conditions include overcrowding, poor water quality, and incompatibility of species.

The physical and behavioral symptoms of flukes are red skin, mucus all over the body or gills, bumping or scratching the body against objects, fins or gills that are eaten up, and rapid movement of gills.

The difference between anchor worms and flukes is that anchor worms protrude into the skin while flukes stick flatly on the skin's surface.

There are medications available in local pet stores such as praziquantel and generic antibiotics. It should be treated with one tablet for every 10 gallons of water.

The second dose must be administered after 48 hours. Do this alongside regular cleaning of water.

Fish Pop-eye

Pop-eye is another common freshwater fish disease that results to one or both eyes bulging out abnormally. A thin layer of skin may appear around the protruding eye.

This skin is a tissue that holds and protects the eye in the socket. As the eye sticks out, the tissue around it will also get stretched.

When the disease becomes worse, fungus infection may begin to appear and the bulging eye may really get shocking to look at.

Fish pop-eye is caused by a bacterial infection commonly brought by poor water quality. Therefore, the first step of treatment is water change.

There are also available medicines such as Tetracycline. It also may be caused by vitamin deficiency.

Supplementing the fish with high-quality food that are rich in vitamins will also help.

Ammonia Poisoning

Fishes that are affected with ammonia poisoning appear to have red and inflamed gills. They are also observed to be running out of breath.

Ammonia poisoning happens when the ammonia level in the water becomes too high. It is often caused by overcrowding in the tank.

When a fish has been diagnosed with this disease, immediately do a 50-60% water change.

Also, treat the water with ammonia treatment products that are widely available in the local pet shops.

To avoid and prevent such disease, make sure that the filtration system is working at its optimum best.

Dropsy

If the fish looks bloated and the scales are raised or protruded, the fish is affected with dropsy. It is not a disease in itself but a symptom of underlying kidney infection.

When the kidney is coated with infection, there would be renal failure and fluid accumulation; hence, the bloating. The fish may also show signs of fading color.

Once the symptoms have been caught, quarantine the fish and treat immediately. Quick actions are necessary as this disease could be fatal.

Purchase antibiotics from a local pet store; those that come in feed and injectable forms are more recommended. It is also better to bath salt the fish.

Along with the medication, ensure the cleanliness of water as untidy environmental conditions may also cause Dropsy. Conduct a 25% water change every other day.

This disease is also associated to weak and malnourished fishes. Therefore, try to improve the fish's quality of food as part of the treatment.

Just like any other pet parent, you surely would want to keep your fishes in their best shape and condition.

Most of the common fish diseases are rooted from parasites and bacteria caused by untidy and unhealthy aquarium environment.

To prevent attracting diseases, ensure cleanliness of the aquarium – the tank, the objects, and especially the water.

To kill the parasites and bacteria that diseased a fish, conducting a saltwater bath would be a good help. Salt is known to kill parasites and fight bacteria that will increase the survival of fish.

To perform a salt bath, prepare a clean bucket. Pour a gallon of water in the bucket; and add 4 tablespoons of aquarium salt.

Dissolve the salt and dip the fish for 5 minutes. Others prefer bathing the fish for 30 minutes; it is perfectly fine but 5 minutes may already be enough.

Chapter 6: What is the Nitrogen Cycle and Why It Matters

Perhaps, the terms Nitrification Process, Biological Cycle, Break-in Cycle, or even Nature's Waste Management System sound familiar to you. It should be as all these terms refer to the Nitrogen Cycle which is vital to fishkeeping. It affects the over-all safety of the entire aquatic community.

An aquarium, no matter how beautiful and well-maintained it looks like, might still be susceptible to toxins and wastes. The fish tank is not an open habitat.

Therefore, the wastes that come from decaying plants, unconsumed feed, and fish manure would just circulate inside the tank.

The good news is that there are types of bacteria that can transform these toxins into beneficial by-products. The bad news is that these bacteria are still not enough.

The wastes inside the aquarium cannot completely go out on its own. In just a short period of time, the tank might transform into something akin to an underground sewage.

To prevent that from happening, you must let Nitrogen Cycle do its work.

As a scientific definition, the Nitrogen Cycle is the process where waste becomes established in the tank; resulting to ammonia. The ammonia converts to nitrite; then, nitrite to nitrate.

These processes are completed through biochemical oxidation. Simply put, it is a natural process of converting waste and toxic compounds into harmless by-products.

There are four steps involved in the completion of the Nitrogen Cycle. The process begins with the decay of fish waste; as well as waste products from dead organisms, plants, and unconsumed feed.

These waste products will break down and produce ammonia which is harmful to the fishes. Ammonia can eat up the oxygen supply and damage the gills.

Next, Nitrosomonas, a particular type of bacteria, will consume and oxidize the ammonia. In the process of ammonia oxidation, another by-product is produced and it is called Nitrite.

The ammonia is no longer present in the aquarium but the Nitrite is another harmful toxin that you should get rid of. Even with just a low level of nitrite can be fatal to fishes.

Soon, Nitrobacter, another type of bacteria, will convert the nitrites into a less harmful chemical called nitrate. Unlike ammonia and nitrite, nitrate is less harmful to the tropical fishes.

However, it can still cause problems to the aquarium especially if it rises to a higher level. This is where the constant water changing comes essential.

Performing water changes will speed up the dilution of nitrate and keep it in normal range.

A new aquarium typically takes 2 to 6 weeks or even 2 months before it can complete the Nitrogen Cycle. However, there are still some factors that can affect the length of the process such as the amount of ammonia produced.

If you really want to speed up the cycle, you may want to add gravel from an established tank. Nitrifying bacteria are already attached in the gravel so you no longer have to wait for bacteria to naturally occur in the tank.

However, be careful in doing this trick as the gravel may also contain unwanted pathogens. Do not borrow gravel from a contaminated tank.

Live plants also use up some nitrates. Therefore, using live plants for freshwater aquarium can help speed up the process.

How to Cycle Your Fish Tank

Cycling with Fishes

In cycling the tank, you may either go fishless or with fish. The latter is not really recommended as exposure to ammonia can be lethal to fishes.

However, if you still want to go cycling with fishes, there are fishes that have stronger immunity. Unfortunately, if you bought the aquarium and fishes at the same time, this is the only option you have.

To start the cycle, populate the aquarium with a good number of fishes to produce waste; most preferably 1-2 fishes for every 10 gallons of water. Do not overpopulate the tank as it may lead to ammonia spike which can be very harmful.

As mentioned, choose those species that can most likely survive the cycle. The good choices include most guppies, white clouds and banded gouramis.

Next, feed the fishes in just small portions and typically once every 2 days. Do not over feed them as doing so may produce more waste even before beneficial bacteria are established in the aquarium.

Conduct water changes; preferable 10-25 % every other day. Add de-chlorinator to the water.

Conduct tests to monitor the levels of ammonia and nitrite. It is recommended to test every day to immediately notice if the levels have already dropped to zero; signifying that the cycles is already finished.

Once the toxins have dropped to zero, you may now gradually introduce more fishes in the tank. But only add a few at a time; preferable one or two pieces.

After the first addition, continue monitoring the water for a week. Be sure that the nitrite and ammonia levels are still low before adding more fishes.

Fishless Cycle

Again, the first goal of the process is to produce ammonia in the tank. Since there are no fishes that will produce waste, rely on the feed.

Pretend that you are feeding fishes in the tank; drop food in the tank like how you would normally feed a fish. The food will soon decay and release ammonia.

Monitor the ammonia level every other day for one week. It should reach a level of 33pm. If it still hasn't, add more feed until it reaches the desired level.

After one week of monitoring the ammonia, test the nitrite level. Once the tank has already got nitrites, it is a signal that the process has continued. Still, continue adding ammonia by putting feed.

After a few weeks, monitor if the nitrite level has dropped. Then, test for the appearance of nitrates. Once there are already nitrates in the tank, it signifies that the cycle has completed.

Then, gradually add the fishes; as similar to the previous method. If you see leftover feed in the substrate, clean them immediately.

How to Test Your Water

During and especially after the Nitrogen Cycle, it is important to regularly test the water to maintain its good quality and ensure the fishes' health. To test the tank's water chemistry, you may purchase water testing kits available in the market.

When we say water chemistry, it refers to the chemical properties or parameters of the aquarium water including the pH level and levels of ammonia, nitrite and nitrate.

For the pH level, the normal range is between 6.5 and 8.2; between 0.0 to 0.25 mg/L for ammonia; between 0.0 to 0.5 mg/L for nitrite; and 0 to 40 mg/L for nitrate.

The test kit is typically consists of test tube, color card, and testing solution. It is important to note that the kit cannot test all the aforementioned chemical properties all at once. You have to use a single kit for each parameter. Nevertheless, you can test only the most important parameters of a freshwater aquarium – pH level, ammonia, nitrite and nitrate – especially for novice hobbyists. There are some brands that offer package test kits so you no longer have to buy piece by piece.

The first step in using the kit is filing the tube with water from the aquarium. Do not dip the tube in the water; use a pipette instead. Fill in the required amount in the test tube.

Then, add three drops of the testing solution in the same test tube. Normally, colored cloud-like foam will form in each drop of the solution

Mix the water and solution well by gently shaking the tube until the texture becomes even and the color becomes uniform.

Simply compare the color of the water in the test tube to the colors in the color chart. The matching color (or whichever color is the closest) reveals the level of the specific chemical that you are testing.

Another way to test the water is by using digital meters. Calibrate the digital tester using a solution included in the purchase.

Then, simply dip it in the tank and it will give you a precise reading. This equipment is the most precise of all but it is really expensive.

If you are on a tight budget, the previously discussed water testing kit will already do fine and nevertheless, accurate.

There are also testers that come in a form of strips. Submerge the strip in the water and watch the color change.

Once the color has been stable, compare it to the given color chart. These are the cheapest water test tool but also the less accurate.

If you do not want to spend time testing the water all by yourself, you may also pour a sample of your water in a clean, air-tight container. You may bring it to your local pet store and have it tested. Almost every pet store conducts water testing for free.

Chapter 7: How to Properly Clean Your Aquarium

Materials Needed

Cleaning the tank is vital in keeping the fishes healthy and happy. In doing so, you will need the following materials.

First off, you will need a bucket. It is better to get a new bucket intended only for aquarium use. Nevertheless, you can also use an old one but be sure to completely and thoroughly clean it.

Other hobbyists keep two aquarium buckets of the same type and size. One bucket can already be used for dechlorinating the replacement water while you are transferring the old aquarium water into the second bucket.

You will also need a siphon for the water and gravel, bleach, razor blade (for acrylic tanks, purchase a plastic one), filter brush, filter media, paper towels and old bath towels. You will also need a glass cleaner or lime remover; be sure to purchase one that is made for aquarium cleaning.

For an algae scraper or pad, there is a wide variety available in the market. Examples are magnetic scrubbers and long-handled scrubbers.

However, remember not to buy from a warehouse or a regular store as their pads may contain chemical residue or soap. Simply buy from a pet store only.

Cleaning the Aquarium

First things first, washing the hands with soap before cleaning the aquarium is not necessary. No matter how much cleansed you think it is, your hands would still have soap residues.

The soap residue might just mix with the tank's water when you intentionally or unintentionally touch it.

There is no need to remove all the water and even the fishes from the tank when cleaning it.

Using an algae pad or scrubber, start cleaning the inner part of the glass tank. If there are still residue that the pad can no longer scrub off, use a razor blade.

Be sure to use a plastic blade if you are cleaning an acrylic tank to avoid scratches.

When done with the inner sides of the tank; clean the decors, artificial plants, or rocks that have already been colonized by algae growth. Remove the objects from the tank first and give it a good scrub using an algae scraper.

Keep in mind that you must never wash the objects with soap. Given these objects' complex surface and edges, soap residue can be very difficult to remove. Just a little trace of any chemical residue can kill the fishes.

If the dirt has been thoroughly stuck in an object and is already difficult to remove by water, you may use bleach instead. Using bleach is safe as long as it is administered correctly.

Prepare a 10 percent bleach solution by mixing it with water in a 1:9 ratio (1 part bleach for every 9 parts of water). Use a clean bucket for the mixture and soak the objects in there for 10-15 minutes.

Give the objects another good scrub before rinsing with water. Then, get rid of remaining bleach residue by drying the objects.

Bleach is an effective algae killer on artificial plants. It can also be used on live plants but be sure to lessen the amount and soaking time.

For live plants, prepare a 5 percent bleach solution and soak for only 2 minutes. Next, use a siphon to thoroughly vacuum the gravel and remove unwanted debris.

Once done with the inner parts of the tank, continue with the light, hood and outside of the glass. Vinegar is recommended in cleaning these parts as other standard lime and glass cleaners contain ammonia.

Vinegar may only be used, though in cleaning the outer parts of the tank. Using it inside can be lethal to the fishes because of its acidic properties.

Simply spray or drop a good amount of vinegar on a clean cloth, and use to it to wipe off the tank. Be sure to rinse the tank walls properly to avoid undesirable effects on water chemistry; you may use hot water in doing so.

When everything is done, put back the plants, rocks, and other decors inside the tank. The next accessory to be cleaned is the filter but wait for another week to do that.

When you cleansed the tank's interior, you have already disturbed the beneficial bacteria present in there. Nevertheless, there are still remaining beneficial bacteria lurking in the filter.

If you immediately clean the filter, you will just disturb the entire ecosystem; which would result to ammonia spike. Let the fishes adapt to their new and cleansed environment first before shocking them once again.

Maintenance

Once done with giving the tank a good clean, make maintenance a part of your fish keeping routine. You can do a weekly 10-15% water change for a regular-sized tank.

If your tank is larger and contains more fishes, conduct a 20-25% water change every week. Going for a 100% water change is a bad idea.

Doing so would only affect the entire water chemistry; resulting to shock and stress to the fishes. Keep in mind that shock can cause death of a fish.

Subtle water changes would help the fishes adapt slowly to the new environment. Keep in mind that simply topping off the water is different from changing the water.

The longest time you could skip a water change is two weeks.

As part of the weekly maintenance, siphon the substrate and remove unwanted debris from the plants. Also, scrape the inside of the glass and wipe off the outside.

Check on the tank on a daily basis to see if there are solid particles, unwanted materials, and fallen leaves that must be cleaned. If you notice that unconsumed food is already piling up, vacuum it using a siphon.

Observe the fishes if they are showing any sign of illness. If so, take immediate action as a diseased fish may affect the entire environment.

Check the thermometer to see if the water temperature is stable. When doing a daily or weekly maintenance, do not touch the filter to avoid disturbing the beneficial bacteria.

Conclusion

One of the biggest misconceptions about fishkeeping is that it is just superficial – buy a tank, fill it in with water and decors, add fishes, and clean once a month.

However, the truth is that fishkeeping is a hobby that involves a good amount of science.

There is a scientific story and factors to consider behind every element involved in a fish tank.

It is, after all, a community of living creatures thriving for a symbiotic relationship.

As similar to any other live community, a fish tank also encounters challenges.

The fishes may get sick, the plants may die, the water chemistry may change, the temperature may drop, and other unwanted environmental conditions may arise.

Since the inhabitants' movement and intellect are limited, humans must act as their community helper.

When problems arise, the fish-keeper must make a move and take necessary actions.

More importantly, he/she must ensure that problems are avoided.

Keeping a fish tank requires patience in the beginning and effort all throughout the community's existence.

Maintenance must be constantly conducted. Keeping a schedule divided into daily, weekly, and monthly tasks would be a big help.

When done right and with a little help from science, fishkeeping can be a delightful and satisfying hobby.

If you make your inhabitants happy and healthy, they will bring you more bliss in return.

Thank you again for reading this book!

Made in the USA
Middletown, DE
28 December 2020